D1174052

our Environment

Rain Forests

Kay Jackson

KIDHAVEN PRESS
A part of Gale, Cengage Learning

GALE
CENGAGE Learning™

Detroit • New York • San Francisco • New Haven, Conn • Waterville, Maine • London

© 2007 Gale, a part of Cengage Learning

For more information, contact
KidHaven Press
27500 Drake Rd.
Farmington Hills, MI 48331-3535
Or you can visit our Internet site at gale.cengage.com

LIBRARY OF CONGRESS CATALOGING-IN-PUBLICATION DATA

Jackson, Kay, 1959–
  Rain forests / by Kay Jackson.
      p. cm. — (Our environment)
  Includes bibliographical references and index.
  ISBN 978-0-7377-3624-3 (hardcover)
  1. Rain forest ecology—Juvenile literature. 2. Rain forests—Juvenile literature. I. Title.
  QH541.5.R27J324 2007
  577.34—dc22

                                                          2007006892

ISBN-10: 0-7377-3624-0

Printed in the United States of America
  4 5 6 7 12 11 10 09 08

contents

A Lost World

Deep in the heart of the Foja Mountains on the tropical island of New Guinea lies a rain forest filled with giant ferns, colorful insects, and strange animals. For centuries, few people walked beneath its towering trees. The people who lived in nearby villages believed the forest to be a special holy place and hardly ever went into it. Then, in 2005 a team of scientists from Australia, the United States, and Indonesia came to explore the mysterious forest.

As the scientists pushed deep into the rain forest, they found plants and animals that had never been identified. The team discovered a small, furry kangaroo that lived in trees and a tiny, smooth-skinned frog smaller than an inch. Many of the forest animals were unafraid of the new visitors. A long-nosed echidna, a mammal that looks like a cross between a sloth and hedgehog, even let scientists pick it up. Curious about the strangers, other animals would wander through the scientists' camp.

This lost world is a wildlife sanctuary. There are no roads through the forest, and no one is allowed to cut down the trees. For now, the Foja Mountain rain forest is safe from the saws and trucks of logging companies. Many of the world's rain forests, though, have not been protected. Each year the forests grow smaller as the need for wood and land keep growing. Scientists, governments, and ordinary people are looking for ways to preserve the rain forests for the future.

This golden-mantled tree kangaroo was discovered by a team of U.S., Australian, and Indonesian scientists on the island of New Guinea in 2005.

chapter one

What Are Rain Forests?

A rain forest is a **biome**, a large area where plants and animals have adapted to live in a certain climate. The rain forest biome is one of the world's oldest. At one time it was also one of the world's largest. Rain forests once covered more than 14 percent of the world's land. Now, they cover only 5 percent.

Just as the name suggests, rain makes this biome different from others. Each day, water in the form of rain, mist, or fog fills these green forests. In warm **tropical** rain forests, downpours can dump 2 inches (5cm) of water in an hour, up to 400 inches (1,016cm) in a year. Cool temperate rain forests might receive about 100 inches (254cm) each year.

Earth's Green Belt

Rain forests circle Earth like a green belt. Most are found near the equator. Over half of all tropical rain forests are found in Central and South America. About one quarter are located in Southeast Asia, and the remaining tropical rain forests are in Africa.

Temperate rain forests stretch along the coasts of temperate regions. The largest temperate rain forests are found along the western coast of North America. They stretch from Oregon to Alaska for 1,200 miles (1,931km). There are a few other temperate rain forests in northern Europe, Japan, New Zealand, and southern Australia. Unlike tropical rain forests, temperate rain forests have distinct seasons.

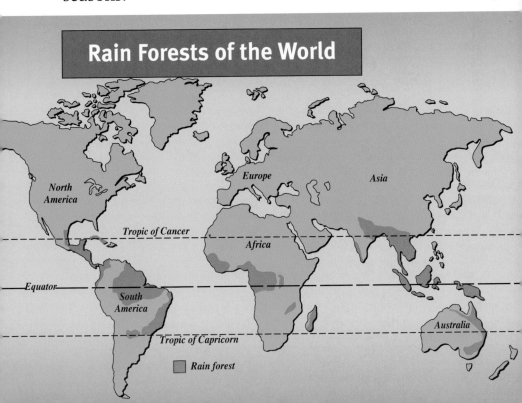

Rain Forests of the World

Europe

Asia

North America

Tropic of Cancer

Africa

Equator

South America

Australia

Tropic of Capricorn

■ Rain forest

Layers of the Rain Forest

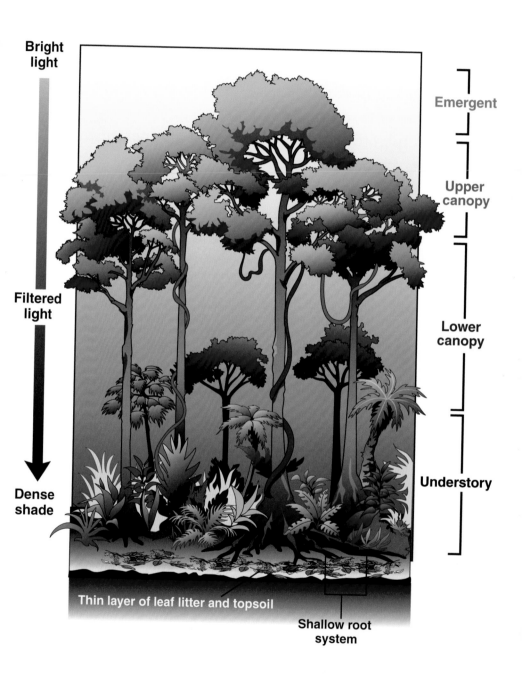

Layers of Life

The rain forest is made up of four very different layers: the forest floor, the understory, the upper canopy, and the emergent layer. At the top of the rain forest is the emergent layer. Emergent trees are 100 to 240 feet (30.5m to 73m) tall. This layer is bright and breezy, catching sunlight and wind. Many trees here have small, pointed leaves and straight, smooth trunks with few branches down below. Birds, small mammals, and any other sun-loving animals live here in the penthouse of the rain forest.

The next layer is the upper canopy where the trees grow to heights between 60 and 130 feet (18 and 40m). Some light reaches the upper canopy, and most of the rain forest's animals live here. Fruits and leaves provide so much food that some animals never go down to the forest floor. They even get their daily supply of water without touching the ground. Monkeys, lemurs, and other tree climbers live here. Bright butterflies and colorful parrots like the macaw fly among the branches of the upper canopy.

Below the upper canopy is the understory. This is a still, shady place. The canopy's leaves block sunlight and wind but they cannot keep out water. Rain slides down branches and trunks. The understory is made of bushes, small trees, and the trunks of taller trees. This part of the rain forest is filled with reptiles and insects. Tiny rain frogs and

The red uakari monkey is found in the Amazon rain forest region of South America and is considered a "near-threatened" species by animal conservation groups.

lizards cling to branches and trunks. They wait silently for their next meal of ants or other insects to crawl past. Some of the world's most dangerous snakes, such as the little fer-de-lance and bushmaster, also live in the understory.

Finally, deep under the trees is the forest floor. Only a little sunlight reaches this hot, dim place. Even so, the forest floor has its own inhabitants.

Beneath the litter of leaves, twigs, and bark that cover the forest floor is an army of decomposers, organisms that break down dead plants and animals. Termites, earthworms, and fungi such as mushrooms thrive in the wet darkness.

With a warm climate, abundant water, and plenty of food, the different layers of the rain forest are home to millions of plants and animals.

Plants and Animals of the Rain Forest

Over time, the rain forest plants and animals have changed to live with a constant supply of water. Some plants have leaves with "drip spouts" that let water run off easily. Others have slick, shiny leaves.

A South American tapir looks for food on the forest floor.

Rain drops slide quickly off their smooth surface. These **adaptations** keep the leaves dry and stop mold or mildew from growing on the leaves.

Plants need sunlight, water, and air to make their own food. In the rain forest there is plenty of water, but sunlight can be scarce below the forest canopy. Tall trees catch the most light. Shorter plants and trees that live at the forest floor or in the understory, on the other hand, have to make do with less light. These plants often have large leaves that spread wide to catch as much sunlight as possible.

Animals have also adapted to the rain forest. High in the canopy, animals like monkeys and

The South American green vinesnake hunts by hanging from branches, waiting for unsuspecting prey to crawl past.

Some chameleon lizards change colors for hunting or protection, which makes them hard to see in the jungle.

sloths climb easily using their strong hands, feet, and sometimes their tails. Large eyes help some animals see through the darkness of the forest floor and understory. Other floor-dwelling animals like tapirs and anteaters sniff and snuffle through the dead leaves looking for food.

Camouflage helps animals to blend in with the branches and leaves of the rain forest trees. A vinesnake is thin and green. It hangs from branches waiting for an unsuspecting insect to crawl past. Some chameleon lizards change colors when the light or temperature changes. Their spotted skin helps them hide from hunters.

The rain forest in the Noel Kempff Mercado National Park is part of the Amazon basin.

Biodiversity

Tropical rain forests have the greatest **biodiversity** of life on Earth. This biome has more different kinds of plants and animals than anywhere else on the planet. In fact, half of all plant and animal species live in rain forests.

A small piece of forest can be home to thousands of plants and animals. In 4 square miles (10 sq. km) of tropical rain forest, scientists found 750 different kinds of trees, four times the number of tree species found in all of North America's forests. A rain forest may even have over 1,000 different kinds of flowering plants. Many different kinds of animals also live in the rain forest. One-third of all bird species live in the Amazon rain forest. In Peru 43 different kinds of ants live on one tree trunk.

Pieces of a Puzzle

The rain forest's plants and animals depend on each other. For example, trees like mangoes and figs depend on the tropical fruit bat to spread their seeds. The bat eats the whole fruit but the seeds pass through it. As the bat flies, it drops the seeds. The seeds have a better chance to sprout farther away from the parent tree. But if the fruit bats were to disappear, the fruits would fall close together. Fewer seeds would grow into trees.

Franquet's fruit bats live high in the rain forest canopy.

Each living thing in a rain forest is like the piece of a jigsaw puzzle. The **extinction** of even one species is like losing a puzzle piece. When a species disappears, the whole picture of the forest is changed. Yet, each year thousands of species are lost as the world's rain forests keep shrinking. Scientists are in a race to study all the new plants and animals that they can find. They know there are more to be discovered each time they trek through the forest.

Rain forests are more than homes to amazing plants and animals. The entire planet depends on the forests.

chapter two

Why Rain Forests Are Important

The world needs its rain forests. Without its green jungles, doctors would lose a valuable source of new medicines, and people would have fewer kinds of foods to eat. Rain forests also clean water and air and keep the planet cool. When forests are cut down, the world's climate could change.

The Lungs of the World

Rain forests play an important part in the planet's ecological health. Scientists often call these forests the "lungs of the world." Tropical rain forests take in large amounts of carbon dioxide, a poisonous gas that mammals and other animals breathe out. When plants make their own food

17

by putting together carbon dioxide, water, and sunlight, they change the carbon dioxide into oxygen and make clean, breathable air for animals. In fact, rain forests make about 40 percent of Earth's oxygen.

Today, experts describe rain forests as the "air conditioners to the world." The green trees and plants of the rain forest soak up heat from the sun. Without the forest cover, the land would send back more heat into the atmosphere and warm the rest of the world. These green belts help cool down the planet.

Not only do rain forests clean the world's air, they can also make clean water for living things to use, including people.

Nature's Rainmaker

A rain forest is nature's rainmaker. Just as Earth does, a rain forest has its own water cycle. Almost every day rain falls over a rain forest. Most drops do not reach the ground. Instead, the leaves of the upper canopy trees catch much of the water. The rest of the rain evaporates in the bright sunlight and forms water vapor.

As the water vapor rises into cooler air, it comes together in small droplets and forms clouds or a steamy haze. Eventually, bigger drops form and fall back into the forest as rain. Some rain forests, such as Costa Rica's Monteverde cloud forest, are almost always wrapped in clouds and mist.

The breathtaking Monteverde cloud forest in Costa Rica.

This blanket of wet air and clouds keeps the rain forest from drying out. The soil on the forest floor is thin and poor. In spots where trees have fallen or been cut down, the sun turns the floor into a hard, cracked surface. The hard soil keeps seeds from sprouting. Without shade to protect them, young trees struggle to grow.

The World's Medicine Cabinet

Besides being a source of clean water and air, the rain forest is like a medicine cabinet. Today, 37 percent of all the medicines prescribed in the United States have ingredients that come from rain forest plants. From stopping simple headaches to curing deadly cancers, common rain forest plants have changed modern medicine.

The rosy periwinkle, a plant found only in Madagascar, is used in the treatment of childhood leukemia.

For hundreds of years, people of the rain forest have used the bark, flowers, and leaves of plants to cure headaches, coughs, and fever. They also use plants to make poisons such as curare to hunt animals. People of the Amazon rain forest would dip the tips of hunting darts in its sticky paste. When the dart struck an animal, it would die in moments.

The curare caused the animal's muscles all over its body, including the lungs, to relax. So, it stopped breathing. In the 1800s doctors noticed that even though breathing stopped, the animal's heart would keep beating. Eventually, scientists used curare to make a muscle relaxant that could be used during operations. Other rain forest plants have also been life savers. The pretty flowering plant called the rosy periwinkle helps cure cancer, a deadly disease.

Off the southeast coast of Africa lies Madagascar, the only place where the rosy periwinkle lives. Two important medicines come from the little plant. One now helps children survive leukemia, a blood disease. At one time only 10 percent of children with leukemia lived. Now, with the help of the rosy periwinkle, 95 percent grow up to be adults.

Over the last 200 years, scientists and doctors have been experimenting with rain forest plants. Their discoveries have saved millions of lives. They have found treatments for cancers, high blood pressure, asthma, and many other illnesses.

An aerial view of the tropical rain forest and beach at Masoala National Park in Madagascar.

Still, few rain forest plants have been studied. More research needs to be done, and quickly, before the plants are lost forever.

The World's Grocery Store

Rain forests are filled with foods that people eat every day. Chocolate comes from the beans of the cacao tree of Central and South American tropical forests. Fruits like bananas, oranges, grapefruit, papayas, and pineapple were first grown in tropical rain forests. Common baking spices such as cinnamon, vanilla, and nutmeg also come from rain forests. Nearly half of the foods in a grocery store probably have an ingredient that began in a rain forest. Some meals may even be made of all rain forest foods.

Each day North Americans sit down to a breakfast of foods that came from the rain forest. Cornflakes, milk, eggs, and coffee can be traced back in time to a rain forest. Corn comes from South America, and dairy cattle were first tamed in the forests of Southeast Asia. Long ago people learned to raise chickens that once roamed the Asian jungles. Coffee came from Ethiopia. Even though it is a desert now, Ethiopia once was covered with green forests.

The rain forest is important to food production. New kinds of plants and animals need to be added to crops and livestock herds. The rain forest can supply the variety needed to keep them strong. For

Chocolate is made from the beans of the cacao tree.

example, a Mexican scientist, Rafael Guzmán, discovered in the rain forest a new species of grass related to modern corn. This new grass can fight off many of the diseases that attack and destroy corn crops each year. Teams of scientists are using the new grass to help grow a disease-resistant type of corn.

Even though the world relies on the things that come from a rain forest, millions of forest acres are cut down and cleared. Scientists are afraid that new medicines might never be discovered. Farmers also may lose the chance to grow better crops. The causes of rain forest destruction have to be better understood so that people can find ways to stop the loss.

chapter three

Causes of Rain Forest Destruction

From an airplane high over a rain forest like Brazil's Amazonia forest, the sea of green trees seems huge and indestructible. But, on closer inspection, plumes of black smoke rise up from the forest, and the sound of chainsaws and bulldozers fills the air. These are signs of **deforestation**.

Vanishing Forests

Each second all over the world, more than 2 acres (0.8ha) of the world's rain forests—the size of two football fields—are cut down or burned. Every year 50,000 square miles (129,000 sq. km) of the rain forest are cut down or burned. That is an area about the size of Louisiana. In Mexico, for example, only 10 percent of the original rain forest is left. In Ghana on the west coast of Africa, only 1 percent of the rain forest survives in a specially protected preserve.

Three hundred years ago there were 4 billion acres of rain forest across the world. Now less than half is left. The planet has lost an area of forest the size of Washington, Idaho, California, Nevada, and Arizona combined.

Almost every threat to the rain forest involves people. Each year more people are born. More people need more space, and much of the world's fastest-growing populations are near rain forests. As the world's population increases, the pressure on the rain forests also grows. People from overcrowded cities move to less crowded rain forest towns and villages.

Slash-and-Burn Farming

Governments often give poor families land in the rain forests to help them start small farms. In Brazil the government encouraged families to move from crowded cities to the rain forest. Thousands settled in the Amazon region. As the people moved into the rain forest, millions of trees were cut to make way for roads, farms, and towns.

Many people believed that it would be easy to grow crops in the rain forest. They thought they could clear the land of trees and then plant crops. Many of the farmers cut down the trees and then burned the slash, or leftover branches

Farmers in Indonesia use the slash-and-burn method to clear fields. The thick, smoky haze drifts over the countryside and often blankets cities, as well.

and trunks. This **slash-and-burn** method causes many problems.

Rain forest soil is thin and poor. It has little topsoil. In some rain forests, the topsoil layer is only 2 or 3 inches (5.1 or 7.6cm) thick while the topsoil in some temperate woodlands is 2 or 3 feet (0.6 or 0.9m) thick. Farmers can grow crops in the thin soil for only a few years. Then they have to move on to a different spot and clear more land.

In a rain forest little sunlight reaches the ground. However, when the trees are cut down, there is no protection from the blazing light and heat. The soil that was once damp and soft bakes under the sun. Only a few hardy weeds can live there.

There are at least 200 million slash-and-burn farmers worldwide. While they cause much of the destruction of rain forests, these families have no other choice. Each day is a struggle to survive. Most cannot afford to buy enough food for their families. They must grow their food or face starvation.

Cattle Ranching

Cattle ranching has also led to the destruction of millions of acres of rain forest. Cows provide meat, an important source of protein. In order to raise cows, land must be cleared so grass can grow in pastures.

Large ranching operations are a major cause of deforestation in Central and South American rain forests.

In the Central and South American rain forests, ranching is the major cause of deforestation. Cattle ranchers in these areas often sell their beef to fast-food restaurants in North America that turn the meat into hamburgers.

Ranchers, however, run into the same problem as the farmers. After about five years the grasses stop growing. Then the ranchers must clear more land.

Logging

The timber trade accounts for 20 percent of rain forest loss. Tropical hardwoods such as mahogany and teak provide valuable wood to lumber compa-

Fire and haze in Indonesia. Oftentimes, logging can contribute to massive forest fires.

nies. Their wood is dense and strong and makes sturdy floors and beautiful furniture. Hardwoods are tough because they grow slowly. It takes hundreds of years for a teak tree to reach its full height.

This slow growth causes a big problem. When a tree is cut down, younger ones cannot grow fast enough to quickly fill in the gap left behind. Much of the exposed soil is washed away by driving rains or blown away by the wind.

Leftover branches and logs become fuel for massive forest fires. Sometimes more forest is lost to fire than to logging. In Indonesia, for example, an enormous fire scorched nearly 6 million acres (2.4 million ha) in 1997. A haze of smoke from the fire covered Indonesia, Malaysia, and Singapore for days.

Technology and Deforestation

Advances in technology have also sped up rain forest destruction. The tools people use to cut down trees have become more efficient.

About 80 years ago, chain saws replaced handheld axes in cutting down trees. It used to take three men an entire day to cut down a tree. Now, one man can drop an enormous forest giant in less than an hour. Entire hillsides of trees can be felled, cleaned, and hauled away in under a day.

Finding a Balance

Both nature and people need the rain forests. Plants and animals are not the only living things that are threatened. Millions of **indigenous** people once made their home in the rain forest. Five hundred years ago more than 6 million people lived in the Brazilian rain forest. Less than 100 years ago, only a million remained. Today, fewer than 250,000 indigenous people are left. Across the world's rain forests, other native cultures are also disappearing along with their forest homes.

chapter Four

Saving the Rain Forests

The world's rain forests provide wood, food, medicine, and land. But they provide more than that. The dense, green forests hold millions of unique life forms, waiting to be discovered. If deforestation continues at its current rate, most of the world's tropical rain forests will be wiped out in this century. This trend, however, can be changed when communities and countries work together to save the world's great forests.

Sustainable Farming

One-third of Earth's land is now used for farming and ranching. As the world's population grows, more land will be needed to grow more crops. Today, the biggest threat to rain forests is the growth of farms and ranches. Runoff water from farms pollutes streams and lakes. Trees are cut down to make room for pastures and fields. Rain washes away bare topsoil. Often the slash-and-burn farmers do not know any other way to farm. But, if their ways of farming and ranching could be changed, more of the rain forest would be saved. **Sustainable** farming is one way to protect the land and help out farmers.

One way to conserve the rain forest is to use sustainable farming methods. Rain forest farmers need to grow crops to feed their families and to

Sustainable farming helps conserve the rain forest by encouraging farmers to leave behind as many trees as possible and to plant new ones to replace any that were cut down.

sell for cash. To meet the needs of people and the forest, sustainable farming encourages farmers to leave behind as many trees as possible on their farms and to plant new ones wherever possible. For example, instead of clear-cutting entire hillsides to plant crops, farmers can leave trees along fence lines and roads as well as buildings. The rain forest farm then has a variety of crops and trees that offer food and shelter for people and animals alike.

Because rain forest soil is poor in nutrients, farmers often rely on fertilizers and pesticides to keep growing crops. Pesticides, or poisons that control insects and other animals that destroy crops, and fertilizers, chemicals that produce bigger or stronger plants, seep into the ground. The chemicals pollute the local groundwater. They can also run off into streams, ponds, and rivers. Fertilizers and pesticides make the water undrinkable for animals or people. In sustainable farming, farmers use fewer chemicals on their fields. They plant crops that can grow best in their environment. An example of sustainable farming that works is the Rainforest Alliance Certification program for coffee.

Certified Coffee

Every day millions of people start the day with a cup of hot coffee. Coffee is so popular that it is the second most traded product in the world. Millions

A "coffee forest" in Camaca, Brazil, where trees protect the land from wind and soil erosion, and their shade protects coffee plants.

more people rely on coffee crops for jobs and income. Coffee used to be grown under tall rain forest trees. In the 1970s farmers began clearing the trees to make room for rows and rows of coffee bushes. With the coffee plants packed close together, insects and diseases could easily and quickly move through a coffee farm. Farmers then had to pour gallons of chemicals on the plants to keep them healthy. These farms grew more coffee beans, but wildlife suffered.

Today, the Rainforest Alliance and the Sustainable Agriculture Network (SAN) work with coffee farmers to grow "coffee forests." Coffee forests are farms where the coffee plants are planted below shade trees. Some farmers try not to depend on just one crop. They plant different kinds of trees, including orange, lemon, and banana trees. Fruits from these trees can also be sold along with the coffee beans. On these farms, few chemicals are used so water supplies are not polluted.

On SAN-certified farms, farmers use methods that do not hurt the rain forest. Instead, wildlife thrives. One certified farm in El Salvador shows how successful this program can be. Rare birds and huge butterflies flit between its 100 different kinds of trees. Deep in the shadows, spotted wild cats called ocelots prowl. A once-endangered giant anteater shuffles along the forest floor while monkeys leap from branch to branch. Certification promises that farms like this will continue to protect the rain forest.

Conserving a Cloud Forest

Many countries with rain forests set aside land for protection. In these **conservation** areas logging, roads, farming, and hunting are banned. However, many rain forest countries are too poor to protect the land. Aid is needed from other countries. International groups give money and knowledge to keep the rain forests safe.

One organization, the Monteverde Conservation League in Costa Rica, manages Bosque Eterno de los Niños (BEN), or the "Children's Eternal Rain Forest." The Costa Rican government owns its famous Monteverde Cloud Forest

Preserve. The Monteverde Conservation League, though, also wanted to protect the lands next to the preserve. They were afraid that pastures and farms would surround the cloud forest and cut it off from the remaining forests. In the 1980s the league started buying land around the preserve. In 1987 the Children's Eternal Rain Forest began with Swedish students studying the rain forest.

Sweden is far from any rain forest. It is closer to the Arctic than the equator, and its dark forests have needles and pinecones instead of leaves. Yet, after learning about the rain forest, a class of elementary students decided to do something to save it. They raised enough money to buy 5 acres (2ha) of land near the Monteverde cloud forest. More children got involved, and soon children all over the world were sending money to buy land. Those small five acres (2ha) have turned into over 54,000 acres (21,862ha) of protected preserve.

A New Kind of Tourist

Millions of people travel around the world looking for adventure. Many look for places where they can see and experience nature up close. Some countries such as Thailand attract these new **ecotourists** with vacation experiences in rain forests.

Thailand has learned to draw in ecotourists with national parks such as Khao Sok National Park. The park's limestone mountains are covered with the world's oldest rain forest. Visitors can

Ecotourists are drawn to the Khao Sok National Park in Thailand for the opportunity to see wildlife up close.

hike through green jungles, paddle canoes on clear rivers, and watch wildlife from rafthouses at the edge of Choi Larn Lake. The government of Thailand has also learned that parks such as Khao Sok must be protected by laws and people. Park rangers work hard at stopping illegal logging and poaching.

Ecotourism can boost local communities. Hotels, restaurants, car rental companies, and tours provide jobs. Ecotourism also educates both the tourists and the people who live in or by the rain forest. When people understand the rain forests, they work to protect them.

Due to loss of land, warfare, and hunting, Sumatran orangutans are a highly endangered species.

Saving What Is Loved

Baba Dioum, an ecologist who studies how plants and animals live together, once said, "In the end we will conserve only what we love. We will love only what we understand. We will understand only what we are taught."[1] To save the world's rain forests, attitudes and practices need to change, and the change starts with education.

One organization that combines educational programs with a Web site is Kids Saving the Rainforest. In 1999 two nine-year-old girls in Costa Rica wanted to raise money to save the tití monkeys and their rain forest home. They began by selling painted rocks. Since then, the girls' organization has grown. Kids Saving the Rainforest has Saturday camps to teach visiting school children about the rain forest. The group's Web site has pages with information and projects that children can do to save the forest. Teaching people far away from rain forests does help but people who live and work in the forest also benefit from education. One group, the Sumatran Orangutan Conservation Programme (SOCP) helps protect endangered orangutans by reaching out to people of all ages.

On the island of Sumatra, north of Australia, Sumatran orangutans live in three small rain forests. Loss of land, warfare, and hunting have left only a few thousand on the island. SOCP wants to teach people about orangutans. Teams travel to villages with puppet shows and games for the children and films for the adults. SOCP has even gone into the war-torn areas to speak to students, veterans, and government officials.

The problems surrounding the world's rain forests are hard and complex. They will not be solved easily. It will take the efforts, money, and knowledge of people everywhere to make sure the rain forests will survive this century.

Notes

Chapter 4: Saving the Rain Forests

1. World of Quotes, December 21, 2006. www. worldofquotes.com/author/BabaDioum/1/index. html.

Glossary

adaptations: Changes over time that help a living thing better survive where it lives.

biodiversity: The number and variety of plants and animals found within a specified geographic region.

biome: A large area where plants and animals have adapted to live in a certain climate.

conservation: Preserving and protecting rivers, forests, and other natural resources through careful management.

deforestation: Cutting down or clearing forests.

ecotourists: Travelers who vacation in places where they can see and experience nature.

extinction: The disappearance forever of a species of plant or animal from the planet.

indigenous: People who have always lived in a particular region.

slash-and-burn: A method of farming used in the tropics in which trees and bushes are cut down and then burned so that crops can be planted.

sustainable: Capable of being continued with minimal long-term effect on the environment.

temperate: A region with a mild climate that is not very hot or cold.

tropical: A region with a hot and humid climate.

For Further Exploration

Books

Lynne Cherry, *The Great Kapok Tree*. San Diego: Harcourt, 1990. Beautiful pictures show the story of the animals of the Brazilian rain forest as they try to convince a man with an ax why it is important to not cut down the kapok tree.

Linda Carlson Johnson, *Rain Forests: A Pro/Con Issue*. Berkeley Heights, NJ: Enslow, 1999. This book focuses on the different issues surrounding rain forest destruction, including land rights of tribal peoples, economic pressures of developing countries, and global warming.

Ted O'Hare, *Vanishing Rain Forests*. Vero Beach, FL: Rourke, 2005. Color photos highlight the problems of deforestation, global warming, and how rain forests affect Earth's weather.

Kristin Joy Pratt, *A Walk in the Rainforest*. Nevada City, CA: Dawn, 1992. An ABC book, each page is filled with colorful illustrations and facts about a plant or animal.

Web Sites

Kids Saving the Rainforest (www.kidssaving therainforest.org). Kids Saving the Rainforest hopes to educate children about the rain forest, protect the títí monkey, and preserve local rain forest land.

The Rainforest Alliance (www.rainforest-alliance. org/index.cfm). The goal of the Rainforest Alliance is "to protect ecosystems and the people and wildlife that depend on them by transforming land-use practices, business practices, and consumer behavior."

What's It Like Where You Live? (www.mbg net.net). Run by the Missouri Botanical Gardens, this Web site has information about the world's terrestrial and aquatic biomes.

Index

Picture credits

About the Author

Kay Jackson lives in Tulsa, Oklahoma. A few years ago she also lived and taught in the countries of Ghana and Colombia. In the Ghanaian rain forest preserve of Kakum, Kay walked on swaying rope bridges stretched between trees more than 100 feet (30.5m) tall. In Colombia, she hiked along ancient mountain trails made by people long before Columbus discovered the New World. Today, only pockets of the once great rain forests of the Andes remain.